W9-ARS-497

After Graduation

AUDIO PRODUCTS BY
ANDREW HORTON:

On-Target Dating

Sticks and Stones

Getting Past Imperfect

After Graduation

Sinking, Swimming, or Walking on Water

Andrew Horton

Covenant Communications, Inc.

Cover illustration by Dani Jones © 2008. For more information go to www.danijones.com
Interior illustrations by Mark Sorenson
Cover design copyrighted 2008 by Covenant Communications, Inc.
Published by Covenant Communications, Inc.
American Fork, Utah

Printed in Canada
First Printing: April 2008

15 14 13 12 11 10 09 08 10 9 8 7 6 5 4 3 2 1

ISBN 10: 1-59811-561-8
ISBN 13: 978-1-59811-561-1

To my wonderful wife, Stephanie,
and my six children, Keena, Malia, Caleb,
Marcus, Kylie, and Quincey,
for their constant love and support
and for making life fun.

Contents

Lord, is it true that a thousand years to me is only a second to you?
Yes, my son.

Lord, is it true that one million dollars to me is only a penny to you?
Yes, my son.

Lord, may I have a PENNY!?!

Yes, my son, just a second.

Chapter 1: It's About Time

You're graduating from high school? Well, it's about time. In fact, it's *all* about time, isn't it? Abraham and Peter said that our time may be a little different from the Lord's:

> And the Lord said unto me, by the Urim and Thummim, that Kolob was after the manner of the Lord, according to its times and seasons in the revolutions thereof; that one revolution was a day unto the Lord, after his manner of reckoning, it being one thousand years according to the time appointed unto that whereon thou standest. This is the reckoning of the Lord's time, according to the reckoning of Kolob. (Abraham 3:4)

> But, beloved, be not ignorant of this one thing, that one day is with the Lord as a thousand years, and a thousand years as one day. (2 Peter 3:8)

Could this be literal? Is a thousand years for us only one day to the Lord? Alma says, "All is as one day with God, and time only is measured unto men" (Alma 40:8). Only the Lord knows. But what if it's true? What if a thousand years to us is only one day to the Lord? If we break it down, it might look something like this:

Our Time		**The Lord's Time**
1000 years	=	1 day
42 years	=	1 hour
1 year	=	1.44 minutes
1 day	=	.24 seconds
1 hour	=	.01 seconds

Seventy-five years is about the current average life expectancy in the United States.[1] Seventy-five years in the Lord's time would be 1 hour and 48 minutes. How strange to think that we will only be on this planet for 1 hour and 48 minutes. It seems a lot longer than that most of

1. See http://www.worldbank.org/depweb/english/modules/social/life/chart1.html

the time. If life will last about 1 hour and 48 minutes, then

- When you graduate from high school, you will be about 26 minutes old
- High school lasts 5.76 minutes
- You will be a teenager for 10.08 minutes
- Prom lasts .05 seconds
- A young man will spend less than 15 seconds in the MTC
- A two-year mission will last 2 minutes and 53 seconds
- Not serving a mission will last forever
- The most important thing that any member of the Church ever does in this world, which is "marry the right person, in the right place, by the right authority,"[2] will take you about .01 seconds
- By the time my wife and I had been married for 17 minutes, we had six children
- You can earn a four-year college degree in 6 minutes
- If you want to be a doctor or a lawyer, you will only need to spend 10 or 12 minutes in college

---

2. Bruce R. McConkie, *Mormon Doctrine* (Salt Lake City: Bookcraft, 1966), 118.

If two thousand years to us is only two days to the Lord, then it was just over two days ago that our Lord and Savior "suffered so much pain, 'indescribable anguish,' and 'overpowering torture' for our sake."[3] It was only two days ago that he suffered "in the Garden of Gethsemane, where He took upon Himself all the sins of all other mortals, [which] caused Him 'to tremble because of pain, and to bleed at every pore, and to suffer both body and spirit.'"[4] Since the Atonement was so recent to the Savior and Heavenly Father, we can be sure that they can truly relate to the temptations, trials, pains, and pressures we experience daily. Maybe this will increase our faith as we pray each day and night that they will "ease the burdens which are put upon [our] shoulders" so that we will know "of a surety that I, the Lord God, do visit my people in their afflictions" (Mosiah 24:14).

If life will only last one hour and forty-eight minutes, then maybe that's why the Lord said, "I would that [ye] should prepare quickly, for the hour [and forty-eight minutes] is close at hand . . ." (Alma 5:29). As a high school graduate, you have

3. James E. Faust, "The Atonement: Our Greatest Hope," *Ensign,* Nov. 2001, 19, quoting John Taylor, *The Mediation and Atonement* (Salt Lake City: Deseret News, 1882), 150.

4. Faust, "The Atonement," 19, quoting D&C 19:18.

used twenty-six minutes of the clock. You are at a crucial time in your life, the clock is ticking, and you may have only an hour or so left. What are you going to do with your time? Elder Robert D. Hales said,

> There is a time and season for all of our decisions. Make sure you make decisions in the proper time and season. All of these life-altering decisions will be made in a very busy, relatively short period during your 20s—during what I call the "Decade of Decision." . . . In the decade ahead, your time for preparation will be limited. . . . You must develop your own preconditioned responses for the important decisions you will make in the next decade of your life. You must know what to do and when to do it when each decision presents itself. Remember that making no decision at all could be just as deadly as making the wrong decision. Many of the decisions you make or don't make will have eternal consequences.[5]

---

5. Robert D. Hales, "To the Aaronic Priesthood: Preparing for the Decade of Decision," *Ensign,* May 2007, 48–49; emphasis added.

The following chart[6] shows how choices made during the "Decade of Decision" truly can carry eternal consequences, such as losing your membership in the Lord's Church:

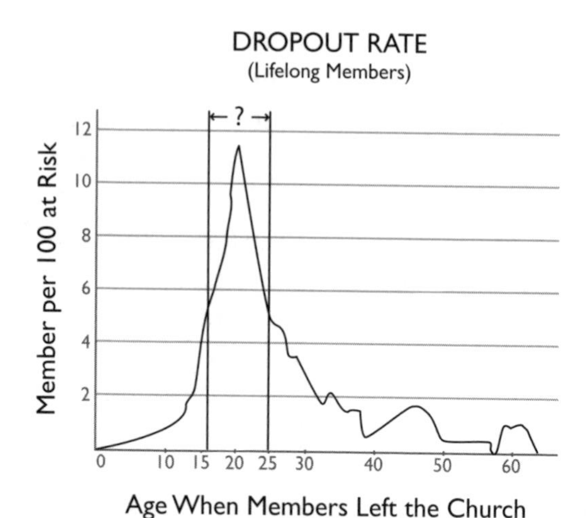

On the left we see how many members are leaving the Church. The bottom displays their age at the time they leave. It appears that the crucial decision-making moments begin right around age sixteen and continue until twenty-five or more. Yikes! As a high school graduate, you are right in the middle of the most crucial decision-

6. Stan L. Albrecht, "The Consequential Dimension of Mormon Religiosity," *BYU Studies* 29, 2 (Spring 1989), 73.

making moments of your eternal existence. The First Presidency has said,

> Our beloved young men and women, we have great confidence in you. You are choice spirits who have come forth in this day when the responsibilities and opportunities, as well as the temptations, are the greatest. You are at the beginning of your journey through this mortal life. Your Heavenly Father wants your life to be joyful and to lead you back into His presence. The decisions you make now will determine much of what will follow during your life and throughout eternity.[7]

It truly is a decade of decision and, in the Lord's time, it will only last about fifteen minutes. What are you going to do with your time?

---

7. "Message from the First Presidency," *For the Strength of Youth: Fulfilling Our Duty to God,* 2.

Chapter 2: The "Big But Zone"

Did you ever have trouble making up your mind? Well, yes and no.

President Brigham Young once stated, "It was revealed to me in the commencement of this Church, that the Church would spread, prosper, grow and extend, and that in proportion to the spread of the Gospel among the nations of the earth, so would the power of Satan rise."[8] As these two great powers have risen, it has become necessary for Latter-day Saints to be able to distinguish the kingdom of God from the kingdom of Satan. Individuals who cannot make that distinction lack absolute commitment to the kingdom of God and are more likely to make bad decisions and occasionally find themselves wedged between

---

8. Brigham Young, in *Journal of Discourses* (London: Latter-day Saints' Book Depot, 1854–86), 13:280.

both kingdoms. The Lord said, "I know thy works, that thou art neither cold nor hot: I would thou wert cold or hot. So then because thou art lukewarm, and neither cold nor hot, I will spue thee out of my mouth" (Revelation 3:15–16).

As youth of the Church, it is especially vital to be firm in your resolution to live the gospel. It is risky to be "lukewarm" at this decision-making time of your life. Being lukewarm makes it easy to give in to temptation when the world offers enticing disguises for the kingdom of the devil—disguises that are specifically designed to lead us away from the Lord's kingdom. Sister Sharon G. Larsen said, "Some would like to live in that eternal city and still keep a 'summer home' in Babylon."[9]

We must be careful and committed. Otherwise it is easy to be tricked into believing that we can draw on the benefits of living in the kingdom of God and still make little jaunts to Babylon, coming and going as we wish. This belief is inconsistent with the teachings of the Church and only leads to trouble and discouragement.

The Lord told Joseph Smith, "For Zion must increase in beauty, and in holiness; her borders

---

9. Sharon G. Larsen, "Agency—A Blessing and a Burden," *Ensign,* Nov. 1999, 12.

must be enlarged; her stakes must be strengthened; yea, verily I say unto you, Zion must arise and put on her beautiful garments" (D&C 82:14). Before challenging the Prophet to gather the Saints and work to strengthen Zion, the Lord warned him that as the borders of Zion increased, so would the borders of the adversary's kingdom: "Therefore, what I say unto one I say unto all: Watch, for the adversary spreadeth his dominions, and darkness reigneth" (D&C 82:5). As darkness spreads, it becomes increasingly dangerous to remain uncommitted to the Lord's kingdom—to be stuck in the danger zone of mediocrity—sometimes choosing good and sometimes evil. Jesus stated, "No man can serve two masters: for either he will hate the one, and love the other; or else he will hold to the one, and despise the other. Ye cannot serve God and mammon" (Matthew 6:24).

A few years ago, while visiting the Hogle Zoo in Salt Lake City, Utah, I encountered a young lady who appeared to be wandering in this zone of mediocrity, or as Joel in the Old Testament calls it, "the valley of decision" (see Joel 3:14). She was probably about sixteen or seventeen years old. She was wearing a red T-shirt that displayed a beer ad on the front. I didn't think anything of it really until the sun reflected off the ring on her finger. She was wearing a CTR ring. Can you see the predicament? If she was a member of the Church, then she knew that drinking alcohol goes against the counsel of a living prophet. So, while she wears a shirt that obviously advertises alcohol, she also wears a CTR ring that reminds her not to drink alcohol. Will she choose the right? Or will she choose the beer? There she is, in the bottom of the "valley of decision," trying to be good and yet advertising the bad at the same time.

A good friend of mine, Blair Van Dyke, refers to this valley as the "big but zone." Those caught between kingdoms often use the word *but* as they rationalize their way back and forth between kingdoms. Listen to some common phrases of those caught in the "big but zone":

- "I need to say my prayers . . . *but* I'm so tired."
- "I should forgive him . . . *but* he was so rude."
- "This isn't very modest . . . *but* it's the style now."
- "We shouldn't be alone like this . . . *but* we'll be really careful."
- "I should stop doing drugs now . . . *but* I will eventually."
- "I should stay for the rest of church . . . *but* it's so boring."

- "I know there will be drinking at the party . . . *but* I won't drink."
- "Yes, I cheated . . . *but* so does everyone else."
- "I need to read my scriptures . . . *but* I have so much homework."
- "I know this movie has bad parts . . . *but* we'll just close our eyes."
- "I want to be good . . . *but* it's so hard."

Do any of these sound familiar? Have you ever used one (or two, or three) of these phrases? Are you stuck in the "big but zone"?

Are there real consequences that come to those stuck in this dilemma? As Sharon G. Larsen taught, "If we are not consciously and deliberately choosing the kingdom of God, we will in fact be moving backwards as the kingdom of God moves forward."[10] Elder Neal A. Maxwell said, "It is so easy to be halfhearted, but this only produces half the growth, half the blessings, and just half a life, really, with more bud than blossom."[11]

Elder Maxwell's words really put this principle into perspective for me. Why would anyone want to avoid the opportunity to blossom? And

---

10. Larsen, "Agency—A Blessing and a Burden," 13.

11. Neal A. Maxwell, "Willing to Submit," *Ensign,* May 1985, 71.

no one wants to experience only half of the blessings life can offer. Imagine rising in the morning and announcing to the world, "Today, I'm going to do exactly half of everything I should do! I'm going to eat half my breakfast. I'm going to take half a shower and get halfway dressed. Then I'm going to drive halfway to work. At the end of the day, I will drive only halfway home." The problem with this last one is that you would never get home! Maybe that's the point. If we live our lives in a halfhearted way, we will never make it back home. Elder Bruce R. McConkie said,

> Lukewarm Saints are damned; unless they repent and become zealous the Lord promised to spue them out of his mouth. (Rev. 3:14–19.) Only the valiant gain celestial salvation; those saints "who are not valiant in the testimony of Jesus" can ascend no higher than the terrestrial world. (D. & C. 76:79.)[12]

Have you ever been "spued"? It doesn't sound fun. Another consequence is defined by President George Albert Smith:

---

12. Bruce R. McConkie, *Doctrinal New Testament Commentary* (Salt Lake City: Bookcraft, 1973), 1:504.

> There is a line of demarkation, well defined, between the Lord's territory and the devil's. If you will stay on the Lord's side of the line you will be under his influence and will have no desire to do wrong; but if you cross to the devil's side of the line one inch, you are in the tempter's power, and if he is successful, you will not be able to think or even reason properly, because you will have lost the spirit of the Lord.[13]

What could be worse than losing the companionship and guidance of the Holy Ghost? These are *very* real consequences for those stuck in the "big but zone." Elder Marvin J. Ashton recounts the story of a five-year-old boy who fell out of bed during the night. When he came crying to his mother's bedside, she asked, "Why did you fall out of bed?" His response was very simple. "I fell out because I wasn't in far enough!"[14] We don't want to be part of the group that falls short of what the Father has planned for us simply because

---

13. George Albert Smith, *Sharing the Gospel with Others,* sel. Preston Nibley (Salt Lake City: Deseret Book, 1948), 42–43.

14. Marvin J. Ashton, "'The Word Is Commitment,'" *Ensign,* Nov. 1983, 63.

we aren't in far enough. At the conclusion of this same talk, Elder Ashton said,

> It has been my experience over the years that, generally speaking, those who fall out of the Church are those who aren't in far enough. . . . The word is *commitment.* To be something, we must be committed. God is our Father. Jesus is our Savior, and this is His Church. May we commit ourselves to living Christlike lives regardless of the environment or opposition.[15]

The key to success is to be valiant in our testimonies of the Savior, "for they who are not valiant in the testimony of Jesus . . . obtain not the crown over the kingdom of our God" (D&C 76:79). We bear testimony of Christ by the decisions we make. Maybe instead of using the word *but* so much when making decisions, we ought to follow the example of Joseph Smith. Watch for the simple word he used in his history:

> While I was laboring under the extreme difficulties caused by the contests of these parties of religionists, I was one day reading the Epistle of James, first chapter and

---

15. Ashton, "'The Word Is Commitment,'" 63.

> fifth verse, which reads: *If any of you lack wisdom, let him ask of God, that giveth to all men liberally, and upbraideth not; and it shall be given him.*
>
> Never did any passage of scripture come with more power to the heart of man than this did at this time to mine. It seemed to enter with great force into every feeling of my heart. I reflected on it again and again, knowing that if any person needed wisdom from God, I did; for how to act I did not know, and unless I could get more wisdom than I then had, I would never know. . . .
>
> At length I came to the conclusion that I must either remain in darkness and confusion, or else I must do as James directs, that is, ask of God. . . .
>
> **So,** in accordance with this, my determination to ask of God, I retired to the woods to make the attempt. (JS—H 1:11–14; bold added).

And the rest is history . . . actually the first part was history too. Anyway, the word is *so.* That is *so* simple. Joseph felt that the right thing to do was to pray, *so,* he did it. What if the Prophet

Joseph Smith had said, "I should go to the woods and pray for an answer, *but* I'm too tired." It's amazing to realize all the good that has come because a fourteen-year-old boy used the word *so.* Be a "so-er!" Second Corinthians 9:6 tells us, "But this I say, He which soweth sparingly shall reap also sparingly; and he which soweth bountifully shall reap also bountifully." Some would say, "sow what?" The answer is, "*sow* righteousness." Here are some examples:

- "I need to say my prayers . . . *so* I will."
- "I should forgive him . . . *so* I will."
- "This isn't very modest . . . *so* I won't wear it."
- "We shouldn't be alone like this . . . *so* we won't."
- "I should stop doing drugs now . . . *so* I will today."
- "I should stay for the rest of church . . . *so* I will."
- "I know there will be drinking at the party . . . *so* I won't go."
- "Yes, I cheated . . . *so* I will fix it."
- "I need to read my scriptures . . . *so* I will."
- "I know this movie has bad parts . . . *so* let's watch a different one."
- "I want to be good . . . *so* I will."

The Savior taught this principle with power in Matthew:

> And, behold, two blind men sitting by the way side, when they heard that Jesus passed by, cried out, saying, Have mercy on us, O Lord, thou Son of David . . . that our eyes may be opened. *So* Jesus had compassion on them, and touched their eyes: and immediately their eyes received sight, and they followed him. (20:30, 33–34; emphasis added)

The Savior saw an opportunity to serve His fellowman, *so* He did. These are great examples of how to *sow* righteousness from the Prophet Joseph Smith and our Lord and Savior Jesus Christ. Let us be *sowers,* "for whatsoever a man soweth, that shall he also reap" (Galatians 6:7).

Chapter 3: Leaving the Ship

Life is full of change. Some things are good to change. It's good to change the oil. It's good to change diapers—in fact, that's good for everyone involved. It's good to change your clothes when they're dirty—didn't your mother always say, "Don't forget to change your underwear"? It's good to change toothbrushes occasionally (not with someone else, but for a new one). It's good to change your direction at times. It's even okay to change your mind. If a bad thought comes into your head, it's really good to change it into a good thought.

Some changes can be very difficult. Changing jobs can be hard. Changing degrees in school can make schooling last a lot longer. Changing homes can be difficult and scary for some. Changing habits is probably one of the hardest changes. Even difficult changes, however, can open your eyes.

A few years ago, I took my family to a water park in Provo, Utah. We had five children at the time, so I was spending a lot of time taking kids down the water slides. Our son Marcus was two years old, and it was his turn to go on an exciting, safe, fun ride with dad. I chose the Tube Run. Little did he know. Little did I know. It was supposedly a simple, trouble-free tube ride, designed for those who wanted a peaceful adventure on a hot summer day—or at least that's how I understood it. They did have signs warning those with heart or back conditions. They just forgot to post signs that said, "You may die on this ride," and "You may come out of the slide with someone other than the person you entered with."

As it became our turn to load into the two-person tube, I sat down in front and strategically positioned Marcus on my lap. I had only brought two arms with me that day, so I wrapped one around Marcus as a seat belt and used the other to hold onto the tube. Down we went. We were having a great time. Marcus was laughing, and I was shrieking with sounds of terror in a joking way—at first. Then I noticed that we were seriously picking up speed. I noticed this mostly on the corners as, with every turn, our tube slid higher up the walls. I still had one arm around Marcus, but I was using the other to try to balance the tube on the turns. We were going so fast now that my pretend shrieks of terror were becoming very real. Life is always scarier when there's a two-year-old on your lap. Marcus was still laughing.

Isn't that how life is? Everything is going just fine and dandy, and then a change comes. I think "flip" is the right word to describe the change that came into my life at that moment. We were turning to the left, but my arm was sticking out to the right. There was nothing I could do. Next thing I knew, I was sitting in the middle of the water slide, holding Marcus and watching our tube jet down without us. I think it looked back and laughed. You're probably thinking, "just slide down!" We would have, but apparently I had on my sandpaper pants. I couldn't get my swimsuit to slide.

This situation wouldn't have been so bad except that we weren't the only ones at the water park that day—we had to share. I suddenly remembered this, and I knew we wouldn't be alone for long. I could just imagine a three-person tube barreling around the corner loaded with large people. In the front would be a woman pregnant with triplets; in the back a BYU linebacker, and in the middle, the linebacker's twin brother, "Tiny." I was sure to get bulldozed and finish the ride on somebody's lap. That would be awkward.

I let out another shriek, stood up, and, still holding Marcus, began to run. Our very lives were at stake. Running on wet plastic isn't the safest thing to do while carrying a two-year-old. I prefer roller blades on cement while holding scissors. I could see our upside-down tube ahead of us. I could also hear screaming behind me—I think it was the pregnant woman having labor pains. I finally reached our tube, flipped it over, and dived in, finishing the ride backwards. Marcus was laughing; I was crying.

So that's how life is: we're sliding along enjoying the ride and the scenery, and suddenly things flip. Our world gets turned upside down and everything changes. They've kicked us out of the boat, so to speak. That's okay, though; you've wanted to get out of the boat for a while anyway. You've wanted to try your own thing, explore the world, reach for the moon.

You may recall the story of Peter and his experience with a boat and some water in the New Testament. The Apostles had been at sea, for some time. As they were trying to get to shore, the wind began to blow against them, as it often does. In the predawn darkness, or the "fourth watch," the Savior came unto them.

> And in the fourth watch of the night Jesus went unto them, walking on the sea.

> And when the disciples saw him walking on the sea, they were troubled, saying, It is a spirit; and they cried out for fear.
>
> But straightway Jesus spake unto them, saying, Be of good cheer; it is I; be not afraid.
>
> And Peter answered him and said, Lord, if it be thou, bid me come unto thee on the water.
>
> And he said, Come. And when Peter was come down out of the ship, he walked on the water, to go to Jesus.
>
> But when he saw the wind boisterous, he was afraid; and beginning to sink, he cried, saying, Lord, save me.
>
> And immediately Jesus stretched forth his hand, and caught him, and said unto him, O thou of little faith, wherefore didst thou doubt? (Matthew 14:25–31)

There is a lot we can learn from Peter's experience. There is even some guidance here for those graduating from high school. Peter left the ship. He didn't fall out of the boat, nor was he thrown off the boat. He *chose* to "come down out of the ship" on his own, just as you have chosen to graduate and move on. It seems to me that the best part of the story comes after Peter, in faith and with confidence, leaves the ship: "And when Peter was come down out of the ship, he walked on the water." Peter was walking on water! He didn't drop off the boat and kick and scream, wondering what to do next. He saw his goal, stepped onto the water, and, as he focused on the Savior, he began to walk.

You are stepping off the boat yourself. Graduation from high school is a step into an exciting new world. You are probably eager to "walk on water" yourself. Actually, you're not just going to walk; you plan to hit the water running. Now would be a good time to chart your path and set some goals. Where do you want to go? Look across the horizon and see what's out there. When you find some things you like, include the Lord in your decisions. Peter did this; he called out to the Lord and said, "Lord, if it be thou, bid me come unto thee on the water." You should talk to your Heavenly Father. Nephi wrote,

> But behold, I say unto you that ye must pray always, and not faint; that ye must not perform any thing unto the Lord save in the first place ye shall pray unto the

> Father in the name of Christ, that he will consecrate thy performance unto thee, that thy performance may be for the welfare of thy soul. (2 Nephi 32:9)

Great blessings will come to you as you include the Lord in your decisions. You will feel much more confident and secure in your decisions when He says to you, as He said to Peter, "Come." President Ezra Taft Benson said,

> By revelation, personal to you, you may discover some of these strengths and weaknesses through a careful and prayerful study of your patriarchal blessing. Through proper prayer you can ask [the Lord] to reveal to you your weaknesses so that you can amend your life. . . . God can reveal to you your talents and your strengths so that you will know upon what you can build. Be assured that in all your righteous endeavors you can say, as Paul said in Philippians, chapter 4, verse 13, "I can do all things through Christ which strengtheneth me."[16]

---

16. Ezra Taft Benson, "In His Steps," fireside address delivered at Brigham Young University, March 4, 1979.

Imagine if Peter had not included the Savior in his experience. When we don't involve the Lord in our endeavors, we will surely sink. Ammon said, "Yea, I know that I am nothing; as to my strength I am weak; therefore I will not boast of myself, but I will boast of my God, for in his strength I can do all things . . ." (Alma 26:12). One of the most important choices you will ever make will be to include the Lord in your choices, especially during this decade of decision, because the decisions you make now will determine whether you will sink, swim, or walk on water for the rest of your life and throughout eternity. What choices did the Savior make that enabled Him to "walk on water" His entire life? President Benson explained,

We follow a perfect leader—not just one who tells us to do what he thinks we should do, but the only one who can say that we should be as He is in everything. In the Book of Mormon, in 3 Nephi, chapter 27, verse 27, the Lord asked the question, "What manner of men ought ye to be?" And then He answered by saying, "Verily I say unto you, even as I am."

What manner of man was Jesus when He was your age—when He was growing into manhood, when He was personally preparing Himself during those thirty years for His three-year public ministry? Turning to the book of Luke in the

New Testament, chapter 2, verse 52, we read these words: "And Jesus increased in wisdom and stature, and in favour with God and man."[17]

These are the four areas in which Jesus grew and prepared Himself for life: in wisdom, in stature, in favor with God, and in favor with man. If we want to walk on water and become more like Him, then we should follow in His footsteps.[18]

17. Benson, "In His Steps."

18. Benson, "In His Steps."

Chapter 4: Wisdom

Our leaders have counseled us concerning the wisdom of getting an education. Elder Robert D. Hales said,

> Get all of the education you can. Decide now to do your best in school and at work. Then, when opportunities knock, you will be ready to open the door and take advantage of them. . . . Develop your gifts and talents. . . . Prayerfully select classes, training programs, and jobs that will prepare you for greater opportunities and more responsibility in the future.[19]

---

19. Robert D. Hales, "To the Aaronic Priesthood: Preparing for the Decade of Decision," *Ensign,* May 2007, 49–50.

Elder Russell M. Nelson said,

> Choose what you will learn and whose purposes you will serve. But don't place all your intellectual eggs in one basket of secular learning. Remember this warning from the Book of Mormon: "O the vainness, and the frailties, and the foolishness of men! When they are learned they think they are wise, and they hearken not unto the counsel of God, for they set it aside, supposing they know of themselves, wherefore, their wisdom is foolishness and it profiteth them not. And they shall perish. But to be learned is good if they hearken unto the counsels of God."
> (2 Ne. 9:28–29).[20]

As Elder Hales taught, education creates opportunity. Education has a definite link to wisdom; however, wisdom and education are not synonymous. President Ezra Taft Benson said that "Wisdom could be considered the proper application of true knowledge."[21] We gain truth through education, and then we use that truth

---

20. Russell M. Nelson, "Where Is Wisdom?" *Ensign,* Nov. 1992, 6–7.

21. Benson, "In His Steps."

properly to direct our lives. This is wisdom. The first question we should ask, though, is where do we go to get true knowledge?

Let's start with the scriptures, in Abraham chapter 3. Remember that time in church when you were thumbing through your scriptures and you found facsimile no. 2 in the Pearl of Great Price? The scriptures don't have a lot of pictures, but you found one—a nice round one with an upside-down cow in the middle of it.

So why is there an upside-down cow there, you ask? Well, I don't know. I do know something about cows though; I know what you call a cow jumping over a barbed-wire fence—Utter disaster. I know what you call a cow that just had a baby—Decaffeinated. That was some useful information, but it doesn't help me understand the cow in facsimile no. 2. The description of the hieroglyphic on the facing page in the scriptures does, though. It describes each image in the circle. The description says the following about figure 5, which is the upside-down cow portion:

> This is one of the governing planets also, and is said by the Egyptians to be the Sun, and to borrow its light from Kolob through the medium of Kae-e-vanrash, which is the grand Key, or, in other words, the governing power, which governs fifteen

> other fixed planets or stars. (Facsimile 2: Explanation)

We have all heard of Kolob because of the hymn, "If You Could Hie to Kolob."[22] The description also mentions "fifteen other fixed planets or stars." It sounds like Kolob governs or guides these fifteen fixed planets. Stay with me now—this sounds deep, but it teaches a very simple principle that you already know to be true. In the verses in Abraham 3, Abraham is shown the stars, which are great in number. These stars are compared to all of Heavenly Father's children. Abraham 3:13 refers to them as "Kokaubeam, which signifies stars, or all the great lights, which were in the firmament of heaven." Abraham 3:3 tells us a little more about that one great star that is nearest to God's throne named "Kolob." Near Kolob are many "great stars" which are called the "governing ones" (see Abraham 3:2–3, and Facsimile 2, Fig. 5).

Let's review. As I understand it, we have Kolob. Then there are fifteen fixed planets, or stars, that are governed by Kolob. Finally, there are the stars in the heavens, which are compared to Heavenly Father's children. All these stars are "very great" (Abraham 3:2).

---

22. See Hymns, no. 284.

You may have already realized the gospel principle being taught here. Jesus Christ, our Savior and Redeemer, governs and directs His Church. He does this by revealing His truths to fifteen men called as prophets, seers, and revelators. Heavenly Father's children, like the stars in the firmament, are led, or governed by, these fifteen men. Wow, what an incredible principle! Let's look at some specific traits.

Some characteristics of Kolob, the Great One:

1. Nearest to the throne of God (see Abr. 3:2)
2. Set to govern all others (see Abr. 3:3)
3. Greatest of all the Kokaubeam (see Abr. 3:16)

4. First creation (Facsimile 2, see Fig. 1)
5. First in government (Facsimile 2, see Fig. 1)
6. Set to give light (see Abr. 3:10; Facsimile 2, Fig. 5)

Some characteristics of the fifteen fixed planets or stars:

1. Near unto Kolob (see Abr. 3:2)
2. Fixed (see Facsimile 2, Fig. 5)
3. These are the governing ones (see. 3:2)
4. Set to give light (see Abr. 3:10)

Some characteristics of the stars, which are great in number:

1. Very great (see Abr. 3:2)
2. Could not see the end (see Abr. 3:12)
3. "He telleth the number of the stars; He calleth them all by their names" (Psalm 147:4)
4. The Primary song, "I am Like a Star Shining Brightly" may have some application here.

The arrangement of these stars mirrors the way that God has structured our world. We have already discussed that God perceives time differently than we do. Each heavenly object also has a different pattern of time. The sun revolves around the center of the galaxy. The earth rotates every twenty-four hours and revolves every year. The moon goes through its phases every month.

The hierarchy of these stars is also important, because just as stars differ in patterns of time, they also differ in intelligence. The Lord says, "I am the Lord thy God, I am more intelligent then they all" (see Abr. 3:19). Kolob is nearest to God's throne, as Jesus is nearest to His Father. Near the Son are the prophets, who are governed by Jesus and receive His light. The Savior shares His intelligence, light, and knowledge with these fifteen men, and they reflect that light and knowledge to us. The wisest thing we can do is to absorb that intelligence, light, and knowledge. Then we can apply it in our daily lives and reflect it to other stars that may need a little more light in their lives.

The book of Abraham teaches us a heavenly object lesson about increasing in wisdom: we must take the truth we receive and apply it in our lives.

A few years ago, I had a seminary student named Julie who faced a wisdom dilemma. We'd been discussing some recent truths given to us by President Hinckley. The counsel he gave was simple: "You are a child of God. Your body is His creation. . . . You do not need to drape rings up and down your ears. One modest pair of earrings is sufficient."[23]

As we discussed this, Julie raised her hand and made a very interesting comment. She said, "Brother Horton, that's hard." I replied, "What's hard?" Julie went on to explain that she always went to church. She went to her Young Women meetings and paid her tithing. She tried to dress modestly, and she obeyed the Word of Wisdom. She said that she tried to do everything she should, but then she said, "But, I really like my earrings." Notice the word *but.* I looked at her ears and thought, *Whoa!* She had multiple earrings running up and down both ears. She was at a "wisdom crossroad." She had received some truth and light about respecting her body. Would she apply it in her life or leave the orbit of the gospel by disobeying that counsel? Would she end up in the "big but zone"? I wasn't sure what to say to Julie because this was such a personal battle she was fighting.

The discussion in class continued, and about five minutes later, a young lady in the back whispered across the room, "Brother Horton, look!" She was pointing to Julie. One by one, Julie was taking her earrings out of her left ear. With a pile

---

23. Gordon B. Hinckley, "A Prophet's Counsel and Prayer for Youth," *Ensign,* Jan. 2001, 7.

of earrings on her desk and one earring remaining in her left ear, she started on her right. The class was silent. When she finished, she had one earring in each ear, and she was staring at the pile on her desk. The class remained silent. They were all staring at Julie, anticipating her next move.

All of a sudden, the young lady in the back stood up from her chair and began to clap. Within seconds, the entire class was standing and clapping, delivering a unanimous ovation. Why were they clapping? Was it because Julie had learned how to take earrings out of her ears? No, they were clapping because she chose to remain in orbit around fifteen brethren and a loving Savior. She hadn't yet won the war, but she'd won this battle. She had received some truth, applied it in her life, and reflected it to others. And she had increased in wisdom.

It was such a thrill for me to see this young lady face a decision like this and then courageously choose the right, regardless of what her peers thought. What a powerful testimony from a young lady trying to increase "in wisdom and stature, and in favour with God and man" (Luke 2:52).

Elder Joseph B. Wirthlin said,

> God opens windows of gospel light and truth by revealing "his secret unto his

servants the prophets." (Amos 3:7.) Those who have "eyes to see, and ears to hear" (Deut. 29:4) can learn eternal principles; view majestic vistas of knowledge, foresight, and wisdom; and receive direction on how to live their lives.[24]

---

24. Joseph B. Wirthlin, "Windows of Light and Truth," *Ensign,* Nov. 1995, 75.

Chapter 5: Stature

There is no question that the health of the body affects the spirit, or the Lord would never have revealed the Word of Wisdom. God has never given any temporal commandments—that which affects our stature affects our soul. There are at least four basic areas which make the difference in your health—in your growing in stature. . . . Righteousness . . . food . . . exercise . . . [and] sleep.[25]

Righteousness

Sin slows us down, spiritually and physically. The scriptures contain many examples of how physical power comes to those that live righteously.

The Book of Mormon testifies often of this truth:

---

25. Benson, "In His Steps."

- "And in the strength of the Lord they did contend against their enemies" (Words of Mormon 1:14)
- "Yea, in the strength of the Lord did we go forth to battle against the Lamanites" (Mosiah 9:17)
- "Nevertheless the Lord did strengthen the hand of the Nephites" (Alma 2:18)
- "The Lord did hear their cries, and did strengthen them" (Alma 2:28)

"On the other hand, unrepented sin can diffuse energy and lead to both mental and physical sickness"[26]:

- "The Spirit of the Lord did not abide in us; therefore we had become weak like unto our brethren" (Mormon 2:26)
- "And also Zeezrom lay sick at Sidom, with a burning fever, which was caused by the great tribulations of his mind on account of his wickedness" (Alma 15:3)

A daily dose of spiritual sit-ups is just as important for our spirits as it is for our bodies. Sit up and read your scriptures. Sit up and say your

26. Benson, "In His Steps."

prayers. Sit up and repent by changing bad habits and calling upon the Lord for forgiveness. Sit up and call your bishop, if necessary. Sit up spiritually and avoid mental and physical sickness. We all need these simple exercises in our lives. The Lord will hear your cries and strengthen you when you keep your spirit healthy. "It does a body good!"

Food

You literally are what you eat; eat good things and you will become a good thing.

While raising six children, I have spent countless hours trying to get my kids to eat their vegetables. Trying to get them to eat is like trying to herd cats. I've promised them everything from big muscles to pet ponies. I've made faces and danced on the table. I've threatened to dump spaghetti down the back of their shorts if they didn't eat it. I can make them laugh and I can make them cry, but for some reason, I can't make them eat their vegetables. I have seen eyes fill with fear at the thought of eating broccoli—I think they really believe they will die if they eat it. I love their avoidance tactics. My daughter Malia will scatter her peas on her plate so it looks like there are fewer of them. Keena, my oldest daughter, will cover her food with a napkin. Sometimes they will even clear their plates when we aren't looking, hoping to escape to the garbage disposal.

One night at dinner, my eight-year-old son, Caleb, was having a hard time eating his potatoes. We had prodded him and encouraged him, but we were getting nowhere. Finally, I said to him in a stern voice, "Caleb, in this family we eat potatoes!" Without any hesitation, Caleb replied, "Well, I don't want to be a part of this family if I have to eat potatoes."

Fortunately, Caleb ate his potatoes and is still a member of our family. Hopefully someday the spaghetti stains will come out and my children's taste buds will mature. I just want them to eat the stuff that has the all the vitamins in it. I just want them to grow up "big and strong," as my mother always put it. And hopefully when that day comes, I won't have a herd of ponies in my backyard.

I wonder if the Lord has similar thoughts as He encourages us to do what's good for us. I've always loved the story of Daniel in the Old Testament. He "purposed in his heart that he would not defile himself with the portion of the king's meat, nor with the wine which he drank: therefore he requested of the prince of the eunuchs that he might not defile himself" (see Daniel 1:8). He was determined to take care of his body. He even issued a challenge to those over him:

> Prove thy servants, I beseech thee, ten days; and let them give us pulse [grain] to eat, and water to drink. Then let our countenances be looked upon before thee, and the countenance of the children that eat of the portion of the king's meat: and as thou seest, deal with thy servants. (Daniel 1:12–13)

The challenge was accepted and "at the end of ten days their countenances appeared fairer . . . than all the children which did eat the portion of the king's meat" (Daniel 1:15). The best part, I think, was the result this diet had on their minds and spirits: "As for these four children, God gave them *knowledge* and *skill* in all *learning* and *wisdom*: and Daniel had *understanding* in all visions and dreams" (Daniel 1:17; emphasis added).

Sister Susan W. Tanner taught us how our spirits can be affected by what we eat:

> I remember an incident in my home growing up when my mother's sensitive spirit was affected by a physical indulgence. She had experimented with a new sweet roll recipe. They were big and rich and yummy—and very filling. Even my teenage brothers couldn't eat more than one. That night at family prayer my

> father called upon Mom to pray. She buried her head and didn't respond. He gently prodded her, "Is something wrong?" Finally she said, "I don't feel very spiritual tonight. I just ate three of those rich sweet rolls."[27]

Surely we have all overdone it at times and felt "unspiritual," like Sister Tanner's mother. Think of the statement, "you are what you eat," and then imagine becoming a sweet roll. Becoming sweet is great, but I don't know about the "roll" part; it does remind me of an experience on my mission, though.

It was Thanksgiving and I was in Palmdale, California. My companion and I, along with two other missionaries, were invited to three Thanksgiving dinner appointments. They were scheduled for 1:00 PM, 3:00 PM, and 5:30 PM. We were growing boys, though, and felt that we needed breakfast too, so we hit the all-you-can-eat breakfast bar at JB's at 11:00 AM. I don't know what we were thinking. We literally rolled away from the restaurant to our first dinner appointment. Then we rolled to the 3:00 appointment. And then we rolled to the 5:30

27. Susan W. Tanner, "The Sanctity of the Body," *Ensign*, Nov. 2005, 13.

appointment. I don't recall ever feeling more unhealthy than I did that night. We laid on the floor of our apartment and moaned all night. No one talked and no one laughed. Nothing was funny. I just remember the pain and the pressure on my stomach. We really became what we ate—two-hundred-pound turkeys.

Great blessings come to those who eat right and respect their bodies. I have said it a hundred times, and I'm sure I will say it again, "Please sit down and eat your vegetables!"

Exercise

Running, jogging, walking, sit-ups, pull-ups, push-ups, weightlifting, or even dancing are all great ways to get exercise. Working-out can be an incredible way to boost our energy, both physically and emotionally.

It's always interesting to do word searches in the scriptures on a computer. It's especially interesting when you type in modern words and see what comes up. I did a scripture search with the word *exercise.* I found that the people in the scriptures exercised many things. They

- exercised dominion
- exercised authority
- exercised lordship
- exercised faith

- exercised diligence
- exercised hatred
- exercised the law
- exercised power
- exercised justice
- exercised control
- exercised conscience
- exercised robbery

Not once does it say that they rolled out of bed and did some exercise. There is no trace of any push-ups, sit-ups, pull-ups, or chin-ups. I couldn't find evidence of anyone running a marathon or swimming the English Channel. I couldn't even find two Nephites doing the fifty-yard dash or having an arm wrestle. This made me laugh because anytime you see a painting depicting a Nephite prophet or warrior, you see muscles. You see a man who has obviously been bench-pressing camels, cumoms, and cumelons (see Ether 9:19). Nephites always look like they are indestructible, with arms and legs as big as tree trunks, but not once do the scriptures say that they exercised.

I did find one scripture that mentions exercise as something you do for your body. It's found in 1 Timothy 4:7–8. It says, "But refuse profane and old wives' fables, and exercise thyself rather unto godliness. For bodily exercise profiteth little: but godliness is profitable unto all things, having promise of the life that now is, and of that which is to come." That made me laugh harder, because now I had finally found one, and it seemed to say that exercise didn't even matter. But then I kept studying. When Paul wrote this letter to Timothy, he was trying to emphasize that no matter what you do for your body, one day your body will be gone. Doing things for your spirit, with godliness as the goal, "is profitable unto all things, having promise of the life that now is, and of that which is to come."

But don't write off all your new year's exercise goals yet. This is one of those times that you don't want to overlook the footnotes. In verse 8, there is a tiny *a* next to the word *little.* Footnote 8a says, "GR a little while." In other words, the Greek translation for *little* is "a little while." To read this verse correctly, it would say, "bodily exercise profiteth a little while." I don't know if Paul meant that it profiteth to exercise a little while each day or that exercise profiteth a little while (until you're dead). Either way, we have evidence from the scriptures that exercise *is* good for us.

One of the Young Women manuals makes it clear that regular exercise is very important:

> Physical fitness improves mental concentration and alertness; it relieves tension

> and anxiety. Some educators believe that students are more alert and attentive when they are in good physical condition and that they learn better. Employers have recognized that an employee's effectiveness is related to physical health. Our physical condition also affects our capacity to respond to others positively.[28]

The manual goes on to suggest three ways exercise can benefit our bodies:

> 1. *Exercise strengthens the muscles.* Strengthening our muscles not only makes us stronger and better-looking, but it also helps our bones maintain their proper position and thus help us maintain correct posture. It also helps keep us limber and helps us avoid the many aches and pains associated with inactivity.
>
> 2. *Exercise affects the metabolism.* Regular exercise burns calories. When regular exercise is combined with good eating habits, it helps us maintain a healthy body weight.

---

28. "Lesson 38: Physical Health," *Young Women Manual 2* (Salt Lake City: The Church of Jesus Christ of Latter-day Saints, 1993), 147.

3. *Exercise improves the nerves.* Exercise can improve body coordination. It can also release nervous tension and help clear the mind. It can also be used as a way to gain a fresh outlook on life and find some relaxation. It has also been known to help people sleep better.[29]

Joe J. Christensen said,

> Choose some sport or other vigorous physical exercise that is consistent with your situation and physical condition and be regular in pursuing it. Get the blood circulating and give your major muscles a workout. An appropriate amount of time and effort spent in exercising will help you to be more effective in all other areas of your life.[30]

So, next to your list of "spiritual exercises," make a list of physical exercises. With some consistency, some motivation, and a little sweat, you will be healthier, you will look better, and, best of all, you will feel better.

---

29. See "Lesson 38: Physical Health," 147.

30. Joe J. Christensen, "Resolutions," fireside address, Brigham Young University, Provo, Utah, January 9, 1994. (http://speeches.byu.edu/reader/reader.php?id=7704)

Sleep

This topic brings us right back to my son Caleb. He walked out of his room one morning after a restful night and announced to the world, "Oh, I slept so good last night; I slept like a baby's bottom." I think he got his similes a bit twisted. Getting kids to bed at night can be a battle, but my wife and I have both learned that it's a battle worth fighting. Staying on a consistent sleep schedule helps the mind and body function to their full potential. My oldest daughters, Keena and Malia, love to stay up late and then sleep in late the next morning. I've noticed, though, that the next day, they tend to wake up wearing their grumpy pants. When they change their sleep cycle from what their bodies are used to, it makes them easily irritable, which isn't a lot of fun for anyone.

A lot of research has been done in the area of sleep deprivation and its effects on our bodies, particularly our brains. According to an article on the WebMD website, "A sleepy person's brain works harder—and accomplishes less. A study using real-time, state-of-the-art imaging shows that sleep deprivation has dramatic effects on the brain and how well it performs."[31] J. Christian Gillin, MD, says,

---

31. Daniel J. DeNoon, "Lack of Sleep Takes Toll on Brain Power," WebMD Medical News, 1.
(http://www.webmd.com/news/20000209/lack-of-sleep-takes-toll-on-brain-power)

"Sleep deprivation is bad for your brain when you are trying to do high-level [thinking] tasks. . . . It may have serious consequences both on performance and on the way your brain functions."[32] Maybe that's why the Lord said, "Cease to sleep longer than is needful; retire to thy bed early, that ye may not be weary; arise early, that your bodies and your *minds* may be invigorated" (D&C 88:124; emphasis added). An article on the American Psychological Association website says research suggests that "lack of sufficient sleep—a rampant problem among teens—appears to put adolescents at risk for cognitive and emotional difficulties, poor school performance, [auto] accidents and psychopathology."[33]

So how much sleep do we need? Jim Horne, PhD, director of the sleep research laboratory at Loughborough University in England, provides a simple answer: "The amount of sleep we require is what we need not to be sleepy in the daytime."[34]

I don't believe that the Lord intended for us to feel tired and worn-out all the time. I would

---

32. J. Christian Gillin, quoted in DeNoon, "Lack of Sleep Takes Toll on Brain Power," 1.

33. Siri Carpenter, "Sleep Deprivation May Be Undermining Teen Health," *Monitor in Psychology* 32, 9 (October 2001). (http://www.apa.org/monitor/oct01/sleepteen.html)

34. Jim Horne, quoted in DeNoon, "Lack of Sleep Takes Toll on Brain Power," 2.

guess that most of us need more sleep. A good friend of mine and long-time neighbor, Amy Lane, uses a phrase each night to get her children to bed, and I think it is good counsel for all ages: "Get your buckets to bed!"

Chapter 6: Favor with God

As we study Peter's experience on the water, it may be easy to overlook a powerful four-word phrase nestled in verse 29. It clearly states what Peter's goal was:

> And Peter answered him and said, Lord, if it be thou, bid me come unto thee on the water. And he said, Come. And when Peter was come down out of the ship, he walked on the water, *to go to Jesus.* (Matthew 14:28–29; emphasis added)

Peter's goal was perfect. He wanted "to go to Jesus." As he stepped out of the comfort of the boat and began this new adventure, he focused on the Savior and literally walked on water. But then the world distracted him, and just for a moment he forgot his goal. President Howard W. Hunter said,

> While [Peter's] eyes were fixed upon the Lord, the wind might toss his hair and the spray might drench his robes, but all was well. Only when with wavering faith he removed his glance from the Master to look at the furious waves and the black gulf beneath him, only then did he begin to sink.[35]

It's so easy to lose focus of what matters the most in life, especially when we change from one phase of life to the next. As you leave the ship at graduation, you will find endless opportunities and adventures calling your name. Whether you are entering college or starting a new job, moving into an apartment, or leaving on a mission, you will experience some "furious waves" and "black gulfs."

In all your efforts to walk on water and succeed in this new adventure, whether the seas are calm or rough, the secret to staying on top of the water is found in the four-word phrase used by Matthew: "to go to Jesus." Remember, the ultimate goal isn't the college diploma or medical school. It isn't the paycheck, the passing grade, or the number of baptisms on your mission. The

---

35. Howard W. Hunter, "The Beacon in the Harbor of Peace," *Ensign,* Nov. 1992, 19.

ultimate goal is to get yourself and those around you "to go to Jesus." When Peter forgot that and removed his focus from Jesus to look at the angry sea and the darkness below, only then did he begin to sink. Paul taught this principle clearly in Ephesians 6:5–7 when he said,

> Servants, be obedient to them that are your masters according to the flesh, with fear and trembling, in singleness of your heart, as unto Christ; Not with eyeservice, as menpleasers; but as the servants of Christ, doing the will of God from the heart; With good will doing service, as to the Lord, and not to men.

Paul taught that we should be focused on the Savior, whatever our job may be. We don't do our work valiantly to please our employer or our teacher. Instead, we believe the Savior to be our employer, and we serve with Him in mind. This principle can be carried into every aspect of our lives. When we study algebra, English, and biology, we can do it to gain more intelligence and, at the same time, to become more like the Savior. Why do we hope for a high-paying job? Jacob 2:19 answers this question: "And after ye have obtained a hope in Christ ye shall obtain riches, if ye seek them; and ye will seek them for the intent to do good—to clothe the naked, and to feed the hungry, and to liberate the captive, and administer relief to the sick and the afflicted." We can learn to think this way about all of the good things we do. Why are we obedient to parents? Do we obey in order to receive rewards such as use of a car or an increase in spending money? Or do we obey out of respect and love, to establish a relationship of trust, and because we have faith that honoring them will bring us closer to God? Paul taught this again in the book of Colossians:

Servants, obey in all things your masters according to the flesh; not with eyeservice, as menpleasers; but in singleness of heart, fearing God:

And whatsoever ye do, do it heartily, as to the Lord, and not unto men;

Knowing that of the Lord ye shall receive the reward of the inheritance: for ye serve the Lord Christ. (Colossians 3:22–24)

The Savior wants to know where our hearts are—He wants to know why we are doing the things we are doing. He wants to know that we know that "this life is the time for men to prepare to meet God; yea, behold the day of this life is the day for men to perform their labors" (Alma 34:32). He knows us because He "looketh on the heart" (1 Samuel 16:7).

President Hunter continued:

> It is my firm belief that if . . . we could, like Peter, fix our eyes on Jesus, we too might walk triumphantly over "the swelling waves of disbelief" and remain "unterrified amid the rising winds of doubt." But if we turn away our eyes from him in whom we must believe, as it is so easy to do and the world is so much tempted to do, if we look to the power and fury of those terrible and destructive elements around us rather than to him who can help and save us, then we shall inevitably sink in a sea of conflict and sorrow and despair.[36]

Many leaders of the Church have taught on this subject. Elder Richard G. Scott said, "Place the Savior, His teachings, and His church at the center of your life. Make sure that all decisions

---

36. Howard W. Hunter, "The Beacon in the Harbor of Peace," *Ensign,* Nov. 1992, 19.

comply with this standard."[37] President Ezra Taft Benson said,

> When we put God first, all other things fall into their proper place or drop out of our lives. Our love of the Lord will govern the claims for our affection, the demands on our time, the interests we pursue, and the order of our priorities. We should put God ahead of *everyone else* in our lives.[38]

One very critical way that you can stay focused "to go to Jesus" is by enrolling and regularly attending an institute class. President Gordon B. Hinckley has said the following,

> In the field of education, we have established the . . . institute program wherever the Church has gone. It is touching for good the lives of students across the world. In the institutes young college-aged students find happy association, they find learning, social experience, and

---

37. Richard G. Scott, "Making the Right Decisions," *Ensign,* May 1991, 34.

38. Ezra Taft Benson, "The Great Commandment—Love the Lord," *Ensign,* May 1988, 4; emphasis in original.

> even husbands and wives within the faith.[39]

What a wonderful and enjoyable way to put God first. Institute classes come in a wide variety of topics such as Presidents of the Church, Preparing for Marriage, and Doctrines of the Gospel. You will find classes that dive into the Book of Mormon and each of the standard works. What an enjoyable way to keep on the strait and narrow course and stay focused in our efforts "to go to Jesus." Just as seminary was a tool to keep us focused in these efforts during high school, institute serves a similar purpose as we move into adulthood.

---

39. Gordon B. Hinckley, "This Great Millenial Year," *Ensign,* Nov. 2000, 67–68.

Chapter 7: Favor with Man

I think it's important to stop here and recognize the order of the last two topics of the four we're studying; first, Jesus increased in favor with God; and second, Jesus increased in favor with man. His Heavenly Father came first, before everything and everyone. You may remember when the Pharisees asked a question of Jesus to tempt Him, saying, "Master, which is the great commandment in the law?" (Matthew 22:36) Jesus' response was carefully worded:

> Thou shalt love the Lord thy God with all thy heart, and with all thy soul, and with all thy mind.
>
> This is the first and great commandment.

> And the second is like unto it, Thou shalt love thy neighbour as thyself. (Matthew 22:37–39)

Aren't these really the same words as "Increased in favour with God and man" placed in the same order? Why is this so important to recognize? Because in the very next verse in Matthew, the Savior says, "On these two commandments hang all the law and the prophets" (Matthew 22:40). Everything we are taught in the gospel falls under one of these two topics. Each of the Ten Commandments instructs us on either how we should treat God or how we should treat our neighbor. Each of our baptismal covenants reminds us either of how to treat God or how to treat our neighbor. And one day you will see that it is the same with the covenants you will make in the temple.

You might say that to "increase in favour with . . . man" is as simple as keeping your baptismal covenants. Alma explained those covenants in Mosiah 18:8–10,

> And it came to pass that he said unto them: Behold, here are the waters of Mormon (for thus were they called) and now, as ye are desirous to come into the fold of God, and to be called his people,

> and are willing to bear one another's burdens, that they may be light;
>
> Yea, and are willing to mourn with those that mourn; yea, and comfort those that stand in need of comfort, and to stand as witnesses of God at all times and in all things, and in all places that ye may be in, even until death, that ye may be redeemed of God, and be numbered with those of the first resurrection, that ye may have eternal life—
>
> Now I say unto you, if this be the desire of your hearts, what have you against being baptized in the name of the Lord, as a witness before him that ye have entered into a covenant with him, that ye will serve him and keep his commandments, that he may pour out his Spirit more abundantly upon you?

According to these verses, those with a desire to come into the fold of God and be called His people are to

1. Bear one another's burdens
2. Mourn with those that mourn

3. Comfort those that stand in need of comfort
4. Stand as witnesses of God at all times and in all things, and in all places that they may be in, even until death
5. Serve the Lord
6. Keep the Lord's commandments

Four of these covenants deal with how we serve our neighbors; the other two deal with how we serve God. And if we are effective in our efforts, then we are promised

1. That we will be redeemed of God
2. That we will be numbered with those of the first resurrection
3. That we will have eternal life
4. That the Lord will more abundantly pour out His Spirit upon us

President Thomas S. Monson once made a statement I have never forgotten. He said, "When we face our Maker, we will not be asked, 'How many positions did you hold,' but rather, 'How many people did you help?'"[40] Those few years right after high school can be very busy and over-

---

40. Thomas S. Monson, quoted in John L. Hart, "'Teacher—You Do Make the Difference,'" *Church News,* Feb. 17, 1990, 7.

whelming. You could easily get so caught up in your own endeavors that you forget to make time for those in need. Look for opportunities to serve, whether at the temple, the cannery, in your ward, or on the bus. Imagine the Lord asking you on a weekly basis, "How many people did you help?" It would be nice to be able to respond, "All that I could." Instead of "increasing *in* favour *with* . . . man," try increasing your favors *for* man. It will make a difference in your life and the lives of those you serve.

I am grateful for my wife's great example. A woman recently called our home in distress over her daughter's birthday. She said she felt that she wouldn't be able to celebrate the birthday at their home in the way she would like because of various problems in their home. She was upset, and her daughter was feeling down as well. Knowing that her daughter was friends with our daughter, my wife said without hesitation, "Why don't we throw a surprise party at my home for your daughter tomorrow night?" I'm sure the woman's heart filled with gratitude as fast as her eyes filled with tears. Through this simple act of service, my wife helped create gratitude in another and at the same time kept her covenants. She had made a difference. She had increased her favors *for* man.

Chapter 8: Stay on the Path and Keep Walking

A few years ago, my wonderful wife, Stephanie, gave me a great birthday present. I'm positive that this was the first time in history this item had been given as a gift. She gave me a very large, orange, steel school-crossing sign. That's right, the one that's shaped like a house and shows two people crossing the street. I was thrilled. You may think this was a strange gift. That's because it *was* a strange gift. It was also very thoughtful. I had been using an image of this sign to teach seminary. The sign contained, what I felt, were the perfect class rules for each of my classes. These rules are great truths for anyone trying to stay on the strait and narrow. Let me list the truths taught by the sign:

1. Get a haircut! I love the clean-shaven, bald look—it matches my own bald head.
2. Ladies first—first, out of respect; and second, you can learn a lot by following the lead of a good, righteous young woman.
3. Keep your scriptures, which are the word of God, close to you at all times.
4. Serve one another.
5. Hands off and no necking. (You've noticed the people on the sign have no hands or necks, right?)
6. Dress modestly.
7. Stay on the path and keep walking.
8. If you do all this, then (notice the sign points upward), you will rise above the world.

Probably the most obvious principle taught as you first look at this sign would be number seven. It illustrates one of the most universal and basic gospel principles: "stay on the strait and narrow path." This principle is taught clearly in the Bible (see Matthew 7:14) and in the Book of Mormon (see 1 Nephi 8). This idea seems to align perfectly with the experience that Peter was having on the Sea of Galilee as he struggled to reach the Savior without sinking.

A few years ago, when I was a fairly new seminary teacher, I had an interesting experience in the classroom. I was teaching 1 Nephi 8, which contains the story of Lehi and his dream of the tree of life. I wanted to teach the story in a way that the students could experience the dream instead of just reading about it. After visiting with another teacher, I decided on my method. I brought to class a sixteen-foot two-by-four and laid it down the middle of the classroom between the desks. Some may not know that a two-by-four really isn't two inches by four inches—although they charge you for the full piece of lumber. It's really only one and a half inches by three and a half inches. Somebody owes me some wood. Anyway, at this point in the experience, I asked for a volunteer; we'll call her Michelle because that was her name. I asked Michelle to stand on the end of the two-by-four, which was lying flat on the ground, and walk to the other end while trying to keep her balance and not fall off (see 1 Nephi 1:22). The goal, of course, was a small tree that I had placed at the end of the two-by-four, representing the tree of life. Michelle began to walk, and by using her arms for balance, she managed to walk the distance without ever falling off. We obviously needed to introduce the "mists of darkness" to make this a little more challenging. I had Michelle come back to the beginning, and we read a little about the dream with the class,

> And it came to pass that they did come forth, and commence in the path which led to the tree.
>
> And it came to pass that there arose a mist of darkness; yea, even an exceedingly great mist of darkness, insomuch that they who had commenced in the path did lose their way, that they wandered off and were lost. (1 Nephi 8:22–23)

I placed a blindfold around Michelle's eyes so that she couldn't see and guided her to the path again. She began to walk, and a horrible thing happened—she lost her balance and fell off the board. Luckily, it was only a one-and-a-half-inch drop and not the full two inches, or she could have really been hurt—I should be thanking the lumber store for keeping part of my wood.

After Michelle fell off, she did what one has to do when he or she falls off the path—she climbed back on. After a few more steps, she fell off again. This happened two or three times until she finally made it to the end of the path. We had a little discussion about what the mists and blindfold really do to us and how it's still possible to make it through these challenges.

At this point in our experience, I asked Michelle to keep the blindfold on and come sit down on the piano bench at the front of the room. I told the class that I was going to pull some things out of my bag of tricks and place them on the path to emphasize the mists of darkness. I told them, however, that they couldn't tell Michelle what the items were or she would never climb back on the path.

I slowly started pulling items out of my bag. Our first item was a thin block of wood with a dozen or so sharp nails poking upward through the wood. This was where the class let out a large gasp—I think one girl nearly passed out. I placed three or four of these nail boards on the path in strategic locations. I also asked Michelle to take her shoes off. Our next items were pieces of glass from a bottle I had broken with a hammer the night before. These also were placed in a few places along the path. My final item really caused some commotion in the classroom—a small muskrat trap that had two half-circles of steel that spring shut to grab the animal's leg. It snaps pretty hard—it will snap a ballpoint pen in half. I carefully set the trap and placed it on the path. (I say "carefully" because it once sprang shut on my finger during a fireside and just about took my finger off. The audience laughed while I bled and cried.)

Now our path was strait, narrow, and loaded with mortal danger. Michelle was shoeless, blindfolded, and ready to make the journey. I asked the class if we were missing anything from Lehi's dream. They told me we needed a rod of iron. I looked around and—to my complete and utter surprise!—I had brought a sixteen-foot metal rod to class. I had three young men come up and hold it three feet off the ground, parallel to the path.

"Michelle," I said, "who in this class would you trust your life to?" She thought for a moment and chose a young man, a priesthood holder from the class. We will call him Dave because that was his name. I informed Dave that he would be representing revelation from the Holy Ghost and that he could say anything he wanted to say to Michelle to help her get to the end of the path safely without stepping on anything. The only rule was that he couldn't touch her because the

Holy Ghost does not have a body. With anything good comes something bad, its opposite, so we needed someone to represent the opposite of revelation. I asked Michelle who in the class reminded her of Satan. Okay, no, I didn't really ask her that; I already had someone in mind. I called him up. We will call him Stan because that was his name. His instructions were simple: he was to stop Michelle from reaching the end of the path by saying anything he wanted, but he couldn't touch her because Satan doesn't have a body.

I gently took Michelle's arm and led her over to the path. She reached for the rod with eagerness; almost a desperation—something I believe we would all do if we really understood how much we need the word of God in our lives. As she grasped the rod with both hands, I noticed how white her knuckles became; she wasn't just holding the rod, it was as Lehi described, she was "clinging to the rod" like her life depended on it.

When I told Michelle that the path was right in front of her, she immediately lifted her foot to take a step. The bad thing was that her foot was dropping right onto a bed of sharp nails. Dave burst out with "stop!" Most of the girls in the class screamed; the boys laughed and cheered. Michelle's foot sat suspended—inches above the nails, and her hands gripped the rod even tighter. Stan was going nuts. He was yelling at Michelle to bring her foot down. "You're fine!" he yelled. "Put your foot down and take another step!" She wasn't moving, not until she heard Dave say, "Bring your foot forward a few inches, and bring it down onto the board, toes only." Fortunately, she was able to tell the difference between "the Spirit's" voice and "Satan's"—something we all need to learn. "Perfect!" Dave told her. "Now, pick up your other foot and bring it forward a little."

Step by step, Michelle, with the help of Dave and a sixteen-foot rod of metal, made her way down the path. She had no idea what dangers she was avoiding by listening to Dave and ignoring Stan, but with the help of the rod, she was able to maintain her balance perfectly. While all this was going on, I was writing down all the things that Dave was saying to Michelle. It was amazing how much they truly sounded like things the Holy Spirit whispers to us. I heard things like, "Stop, back a little, forward a little, careful, don't step there, good job, that's gonna leave a mark, slow down, and watch out!"

Life can be tricky. Right when we seem to be gliding along in life so perfectly, taking steps down the path, we get a little confident in ourselves, we forget to listen to the voices that matter, and whamo! We mess up. This happened to Michelle. She got trucking down the path, and I think she was feeling a little too sure of herself, because for some reason she didn't listen to what Dave said and "SNAP!" She found the muskrat trap. It closed on her foot, she screamed, and the class went silent.

(This probably sounds really bad, but it didn't hurt her—she screamed because of the noise it made and because she didn't know what it was; remember, she was blindfolded. You should know that the trap couldn't have hurt her foot as much as it hurt my finger. The trap only hurts if it builds up some velocity and snaps on something thin, like a finger or a ballpoint pen. Feet are thick, so the trap didn't snap nearly as hard on Michelle's foot as it did on my finger. It still scared her, though, which was why she screamed.)

And for some reason, she left it clamped onto her sock. It had a small chain attached to the end of the trap, so that with every step she took, it rattled and banged against everything in her path. It seemed to keep her from focusing on the correct voice, and also made it a challenge to walk normally. It also was distracting for the rest of us as we observed; it became almost the only thing we noticed about her.

Michelle made her way down the path, avoiding the glass and the nails and eventually making it to the end of the path. The first thing she did when she stepped off the end of the board was take off her blindfold. The second thing she did was punch me in the arm; so I punched her back—just kidding. She punched me and yelled, "Brother Horton, I could have really gotten hurt!" This was the topic of our discussion for the next few minutes, because it really is true of our existence here on earth. Walking the path everyday can be a real challenge, and we really could get hurt if we don't use the tools the Lord has given us. I'm sure we knew this, and so did our Heavenly Father, when we left His presence.

Peter was walking on the sea just fine until he got distracted by the wind and the waves around him, and then he began to sink. Fortunately, the Savior "stretched forth his hand and caught him" (Matthew 14:30), then all was well. Like Michelle and Peter, each of us will have moments when we stumble and start to sink, but if we rely on the Savior, we can still complete our journeys safely. Of course, the choices we make have a great deal to do with how difficult those journeys will be. What if Peter had had a steel trap stuck to his foot? He surely would have sunk a lot faster, and it surely would have been a lot more difficult to walk on water.

Too many of us have these traps stuck on our feet. They come in many forms, such as immorality, immodesty, lying, backbiting, cheating, stealing, pride, and guilt. Some carry the trap of being unforgiving toward someone who has offended them, and some carry the trap of being unwilling to forgive themselves of sins they have already repented of. Others are burdened by the horrible trap of addiction. These are the traps of mortality, and at some time or another we are all burdened by them_the secret is to ask for help in removing them. Bishops are willing to help and can offer great counsel to help us reach the Savior and have our burdens lightened. The Savior said,

> Come unto me, all ye that labour and are heavy laden, and I will give you rest. Take my yoke upon you, and learn of me; for I am meek and lowly in heart: and ye shall find rest unto your souls. For my yoke is easy, and my burden is light. (Matthew 11:28–30)

In Mosiah 24:14–15, the Lord said,

> And I will also ease the burdens which are put upon your shoulders, that even you cannot feel them upon your backs, even while you are in bondage; and this will I do that ye may stand as witnesses for me hereafter, and that ye may know of a surety that I, the Lord God, do visit my people in their afflictions.

> And now it came to pass that the burdens which were laid upon Alma and his brethren were made light; yea, the Lord did strengthen them that they could bear up their burdens with ease, and they did submit cheerfully and with patience to all the will of the Lord.

Two things grab my attention in these scriptures; first of all, the Lord will truly help remove the traps and chains with which we are bound. I have a testimony of this because of personal sacred experiences that I have had in my life. Second, both scriptures teach what happens to the burdens once we invite the Lord into the problem: the burdens become light.

If we look up the word *light* in the scriptures, we find a few synonyms. My favorite is the word *intelligence.* What happens as the Lord lightens our load? The burdens become intelligence; we gain a testimony and knowledge that the Lord lives and will help us walk the path, whatever that path is. "The burdens which were laid upon Alma and his brethren were made [intelligence]" (Mosiah 24:15). Maybe that's why Mosiah 24:14 says, ". . . *that ye may know* of a surety that I, the Lord God, do visit my people in their afflictions." They came to know; they gained a testimony.

I asked Michelle after this experience which was more important to help her down the path, a rod to hold onto (the word of God), or Dave (revelation from the Holy Ghost) providing inspiration along the way. It was a question that Michelle couldn't answer. Both were essential tools for navigating a dangerous journey. I am grateful for the word of God and the Holy Ghost which lead me and guide me along my mortal path. I am grateful for the hand of God that stretches forth and catches me each time the winds and the waves rise up around me.

When I think back to my years in college, it seems like I was always doing homework. If there was ever a moment when I wasn't doing homework, I was working. I was studying for a degree in zoology at BYU, teaching seminary part-time, and working at a credit union full-time. Life was consuming me, and it seemed like I never, ever had enough time. I believe it is good to stay busy because it keeps us out of trouble. At the same time, though, life can become overwhelming—our bodies get tired and feelings of discouragement seem to creep in. The adversary loves this and seeks to wear us down physically and spiritually.

I have always loved Elder Jeffrey R. Holland of the Quorum of the Twelve Apostles. In 1999, he shared a story in general conference about his car breaking down, twice, in the same spot, on the same day, when he and his wife and children were trying to drive a great distance. I remember listening to his experience because it was a Saturday and I was in my garage, wearing a tool belt, trying to fix something. I think it was the first time I've ever shed tears while wearing a tool belt. Well, that's not true—I've shed many tears while in a tool belt . . . but not for the same reason. I was a young father and could relate to his experience. It gave me great encouragement at a time when life was a bit of a challenge. The story was great, but what I really appreciated were his concluding words of encouragement.

> Just two weeks ago this weekend, I drove by that exact spot. . . . That same beautiful and loyal wife, my dearest friend and greatest supporter for all these years, was curled up asleep in the seat beside me. . . . The automobile we were driving this time was modest but very pleasant and very safe. . . . in my mind's eye, for just an instant, I thought perhaps I saw on that side road . . . a young fellow walking toward Kanarraville, with plenty of distance still ahead of him. His shoulders seemed to be slumping a little, the weight of a young father's fear evident in his

> pace. In the scriptural phrase his hands did seem to "hang down." In that imaginary instant, I couldn't help calling out to him: Don't give up, boy. Don't you quit. You keep walking. You keep trying. There is help and happiness ahead. . . . You keep your chin up. It will be all right in the end. Trust God and believe in good things to come.[41]

These words struck my heart. They were true, direct, and encouraging. They were the words of a wise father and husband. But more than that, they were the wise, prophetic words of an inspired, living prophet of God, so I knew they were true.

We are all faced with the fourfold challenge to increase our wisdom, stature, favor with God, and favor with man. I've never literally walked on water as Peter and the Savior did. I have learned, however, that when I place my faith and trust in the Savior, I can do some pretty amazing things. I try to remember the words of Ammon often: "In his [God's] strength I can do all things" (Alma 26:12). I know the same thing that every high school graduate should know: There is help and

---

41. Jeffrey R. Holland, "'An High Priest of Good Things to Come,'" *Ensign,* Nov. 1999, 36.

happiness ahead—a lot of it. If you will keep trying, keep walking, and keep your chin up, things will be all right in the end. Place your trust in God and always believe that there are good things to come.

A Summary

1. **It's about time**—Use your time wisely because 1 hour and 48 minutes isn't very long.
2. **But!**—Practice using the word *SO* instead.
3. **Leaving the Ship**—As you leave the ship, it's okay to want to walk on water, but include the Lord in your many decisions and adventures.
4. **Increase in wisdom**—Get some truth and apply it your life. Stay in orbit!
5. **Increase in stature**—Live righteously, eat, exercise, and don't forget to sleep.
6. **Increase in favor with God**—Stay focused "to go to Jesus" by putting Him and your Heavenly Father first in all things.
7. **Increase in favor with man**—Keep your baptismal covenants by recognizing the needs of others and by serving them.
8. **Stay on the path and keep walking**—Place your trust in God and believe in good things to come.

About the Author

Andrew Horton holds a bachelor's degree in Zoology from Brigham Young University and a master's degree in education from the University of Phoenix. He served a Spanish-speaking mission to San Bernardino, California, and then in 1995 he was hired as a seminary teacher by the Church Educational System. He also spent a few years at the Church Office Building, where he helped develop media for seminary and institute classrooms. Andrew loves teaching the youth in seminary classes, and he also enjoys teaching older students in institute classes and in Continuing Education classes at Brigham Young University.